BETWEEN SETS

A MINDFULNESS PRACTICE FOR SURFERS

QUINN PATH

Copyright © 2026 by Quinn Path

All rights reserved.

No part of this book may be reproduced in any form or by any electronic or mechanical means, including information storage and retrieval systems, without written permission from the author, except for brief quotations in reviews.

Published by Pana Mind Press

CONTENTS

1. Introduction — 1
2. Between Sets — 5
3. Noticing the Horizon — 9
4. When the Mind Gets Busy — 14
5. The Body on the Board — 18
6. Missing Waves — 24
7. Short Moments Count — 30
8. Letting Waves Go — 35
9. Forgetting and Remembering — 40
10. The Moment Before Paddling — 45
11. When Nothing Is Happening — 50
12. What Carries Over — 55
13. Staying With What Is — 59
14. A Note to Readers — 63

1
INTRODUCTION

Surfing brings certain things into view straight away.

Waiting.

Timing.

Fear.

Hesitation.

Moments where there's no time to think.

None of this is theoretical. You feel it in your body, in your breath, and in where your attention goes. When you're in the water, it's hard to avoid noticing these things, even if you don't have words for them yet.

This book exists to put words to that experience.

It's not a book about surfing technique. It won't tell you how to paddle better, position yourself, or choose waves. It's not about improving performance or learning how to control fear. There are no breathing drills, mental tricks, or strategies for staying calm under pressure.

Instead, it looks at something simpler.

It looks at attention.

Attention is always active in the water. It scans the horizon. It tracks movement. It reacts to changes. It tightens when something matters and loosens when it doesn't. Fear, excitement, and hesitation all move through it.

Most of the time, attention is so busy doing its job that you don't notice it. You usually become aware of it only after it has already carried you somewhere, into a thought, a reaction, or a decision that feels sudden.

Surfing makes this easier to see.

There's a lot of waiting, so attention has fewer places to hide. Timing matters, so hesitation stands out. Fear shows up clearly, and the body often reacts before the mind has time to explain what's happening.

This book is an invitation to notice those moments more closely.

Not to change them.

Not to manage them.

Just to recognize them as they happen.

The practices in this book are intentionally small. Each chapter ends with a one-minute practice. They're simply chances to look more carefully at what's already going on.

You don't need to sit in a certain way.

You don't need to breathe differently.

You don't need to be calm, focused, or prepared.

The only thing required is a willingness to notice.

If attention drifts, that's noticed.

If fear shows up, that's noticed.

If you forget completely and only realise later, that realisation is noticed too.

Nothing needs fixing.

This approach might feel unfamiliar. A lot of books about fear, focus, or mindset are written with a clear goal. They aim to regulate emotions, sharpen concentration, or help you stay calm under pressure.

This book takes a different approach.

It doesn't treat fear as something to overcome. It treats fear as something that appears naturally when something matters. It doesn't treat attention as a tool to be used. It treats attention as already working, whether you're aware of it or not.

Because of that, the book doesn't promise specific results.

It doesn't promise better surfing.

It doesn't promise confidence or calm.

It doesn't promise longer breath holds or better decisions.

What it offers is familiarity.

When fear, excitement, or hesitation stop being surprising, they usually take up less space. Less energy goes into reacting to them. Less effort goes into managing what's already happening.

Over time, this changes how time in the water feels. Not because anything new is added, but because something unnecessary starts to fall away.

The chapters that follow move slowly. They begin with waiting, with nothing happening, and with moments that are easy to miss. From there, they move into hesitation, commitment, fear, and breath. Eventually, they return to waiting again, and to how what you learn in the water carries into everyday life.

You don't need to read this book in a particular way. You can read one chapter at a time. You can skip around. You can ignore the practices and come back to them later.

There's nothing to complete.

Surfing doesn't reward forcing, and neither does this book.

If something here feels familiar, that's enough. If something doesn't land, it can be left aside. Attention doesn't need agreement to be noticed.

The book begins the same way many surf sessions do.

In the space where nothing seems to be happening.

Between sets.

2

BETWEEN SETS

Most of surfing doesn't happen on the wave.

It happens in the waiting.

You sit on the board and watch the horizon. The water shifts underneath you. Sets roll through. Sometimes nothing happens for a long time. Other times, everything changes in a few seconds.

The space between waves is easy to dismiss. It can feel like downtime, something to endure before the real part starts. But it's also where attention is most easily noticed.

When you're waiting, there isn't much to do. No movements to plan. No decisions to make. Attention shows itself without needing anything from you.

You might notice it scanning the horizon, then drifting into thoughts about the last wave. You might notice impatience, anticipation, or boredom. You might notice the body adjusting on the board without any conscious choice.

None of this needs fixing.

Between sets, attention is already doing its thing. It shifts, pauses, tightens, and relaxes on its own. The practice isn't to control it. It's to notice that it's moving at all.

A lot of people think meditation needs quiet, stillness, or a certain posture. But attention doesn't wait for perfect conditions. It becomes most obvious when there's nothing else competing for it.

Waiting in the water is one of those moments.

When no waves are coming, the mind fills the space. Thoughts show up more often. Time can feel slower. Small sensations stand out. At first, this can feel uncomfortable, especially if you're used to being busy.

That discomfort isn't a problem.

It's just the absence of distraction.

In everyday life, attention is almost always occupied. There's always something to check, respond to, or think about. A lot of what's happening inside goes unnoticed because attention keeps being pulled outward.

Between sets, those pulls ease off.

With fewer demands, attention turns back on itself. You start to see how often it moves, how quickly it reacts, and how easily it gets caught up in expectation.

That doesn't mean you're doing anything wrong. It means you're seeing more clearly.

You don't need to hold attention on the horizon.

You don't need to keep it steady.

You don't need to stop thinking or wait for the right moment.

If attention wanders, notice that.

If it comes back to the water, notice that too.

If you realise you've been lost in thought for a while, that realisation is part of it.

Nothing has been missed.

Between sets, there's no goal to reach and no wave to chase. There's just the simple fact of sitting in the water and noticing how attention behaves when it isn't being used for anything in particular.

This kind of noticing won't make the next wave arrive any faster. But over time, it does change how waiting feels. Attention starts to be recognised as it moves, instead of only being noticed after it's already carried you away.

That recognition is quiet.

It doesn't feel special.

That ordinariness matters.

Surfing doesn't wait for perfect focus. Waves come whether you're calm or distracted, patient or restless. The ocean doesn't ask you to be ready.

Between sets, you're already in the experience. Attention is already working. The practice is simply to see that this is happening.

The rest of the book returns to this again and again, in different ways and at different moments. But it always starts here, in the space where nothing seems to be happening, and attention has nowhere special to go.

That space isn't empty.

It's where noticing begins.

One-Minute Practice

You can do this sitting in the water, or anywhere else.

QUINN PATH

For one minute, don't try to focus on anything in particular.

Just notice what attention is already doing.

You might notice it scanning the horizon.

You might notice it drifting into thought.

You might notice sensations in the body or sounds around you.

There's nothing to hold onto.

If attention moves, let it move.

If you forget and realise later, notice that realisation.

When the minute is over, stop. No judging how it went.

3
NOTICING THE HORIZON

When you're sitting in the water, the horizon naturally becomes a reference point.

It stretches across your view, steady and distant. Waves rise and fall in front of it. Sets approach, then pass. The horizon itself stays the same while everything else moves around it.

Most surfers spend a lot of time looking toward the horizon. You scan for incoming sets. You watch spacing, shape, and movement. That's practical. It's part of being in the water.

But there's something else happening at the same time.

Without really noticing, attention is constantly adjusting. It opens out, then narrows. It moves from the horizon to the water nearby, from distant movement to the feel of the board underneath you. Sometimes it's steady. Other times, it jumps quickly from one thing to another.

This chapter isn't about learning to read waves better.

It's about noticing how attention behaves while you're already looking.

There's a difference between looking and searching.

Searching has an aim. It's trying to find something specific. It carries a bit of tension because attention measures what's there against what it hopes will happen next. When you're searching, attention tightens.

Looking is different. The field of view stays open. The horizon is still there, but attention isn't straining toward it. Movement is noticed as it appears, without needing to decide straight away what it means.

Most of the time, attention shifts between these two without you realising.

You might scan intently for a while, then soften into a wider awareness where the water, sky, and body are all present at once. Then, suddenly, attention tightens again, pulled by anticipation or impatience.

None of this is a mistake.

The point isn't to stay in one mode or the other. The point is simply to notice that these shifts are happening.

When attention goes unnoticed, it feels like you're just looking at the horizon. When attention is noticed, you start to see how quickly it reacts to expectation.

A set appears in the distance. Attention sharpens. The body becomes alert. The breath might shorten slightly. Thoughts jump ahead of the moment.

That reaction is automatic.

It doesn't need to be stopped.

What matters is whether it's seen.

When you notice attention tightening, it has less pull. It still responds, but it doesn't drag you fully into tension or prediction. There's a bit more space around the reaction.

That space doesn't come from effort.

It appears when the shift is noticed early.

A lot of surfers think they're either focused or distracted, as if attention switches on and off. But attention is always there. What changes is how it moves and what it locks onto.

Sometimes attention is wide. The horizon, the sound of the water, the movement of the board, and balance are all there together. Other times, attention narrows onto one detail.

Both are natural.

Problems only show up when these movements go unnoticed. When attention narrows without being seen, it can rush you forward. When it widens without being noticed, it can drift into dullness.

Noticing brings both into view.

The horizon helps because it's always there and mostly unchanged. It doesn't demand anything. It gives attention something stable to relate to.

You can notice how often your gaze rests there without effort. You can also notice how often it tightens into searching, especially during long waits.

You don't need to hold your gaze anywhere.

You're free to look around.

You're free to drift.

You're free to lose attention completely and realise it later.

Every realisation counts.

Over time, the difference between looking and searching becomes easier to feel. You may notice tension earlier. You may sense anticipation before it fully takes over. You may see how quickly attention jumps ahead of what's actually happening.

Again, nothing needs fixing.

Surfing doesn't reward constant prediction. It rewards responsiveness. Attention that's allowed to move naturally, while being noticed as it moves, is often more responsive than attention that's tightly controlled.

This doesn't only apply to the horizon.

The same pattern shows up in everyday life. Waiting in line. Watching traffic lights. Listening to someone talk. Attention shifts between open awareness and narrow focus, between looking and searching.

The water makes this easier to see because there's not much else to do.

You're not trying to calm your mind when you notice these shifts. You're just getting familiar with how attention behaves when it's allowed to do what it already does.

That familiarity matters.

When attention is familiar, it surprises you less. When it surprises you less, it interferes less. You respond to what's happening, not to what you think might happen next.

This isn't something you finish. It's something you notice again and again, in small moments, without keeping track.

The horizon will still be there.

Sets will still come and go.

Attention will still move as it always has.

The difference is that you start to see that movement as it happens.

One-Minute Practice

For one minute, let your gaze rest naturally.

It might rest on the horizon, the water nearby, or something else entirely.

Don't try to hold attention anywhere.

Don't search for movement.

Don't try to stay wide or focused.

Notice when attention softens.

Notice when it tightens.

Notice when it drifts and when it comes back.

If you realise you've been lost in thought, notice that realisation.

When the minute is over, stop. No deciding whether attention did it "right."

4

WHEN THE MIND GETS BUSY

Most surfers notice that their mind gets busier the longer they sit out the back.

Thoughts pile up. The wait feels longer. The sitting can start to feel heavier than the paddling or the wave itself.

That can be confusing, because nothing much is happening. The water is calm. You're not making decisions. You're just waiting. And yet the mind starts to feel noisy or unsettled.

This doesn't mean the mind has suddenly switched on.

It means there's less to distract it.

When you're not moving or reacting, thoughts are easier to notice. The mind starts commenting. Wondering when the next set will come. Replaying earlier waves. Making up little plans that don't go anywhere.

That's normal.

What's different is that you're actually seeing it.

A lot of people take this as a bad sign. It can feel like you're getting more distracted instead of more focused. But it's usually the opposite. You're just noticing what's been running in the background the whole time.

That's not a problem with attention.

It's a clearer view of how attention works.

The usual reaction is to try to fix it. You might stare harder at the horizon, keep scanning, or look for something to do so the noise settles down.

That just adds more activity. Instead of noticing thought, you end up managing it.

This chapter isn't asking you to stop thinking.

It's asking you to notice the thinking as it happens.

This is easier to spot in the water.

When the mind is busy, it often creates a low-level urgency. It can feel like something should be happening, even when the ocean is quiet. You might feel restless for no clear reason.

That feeling isn't caused by thought itself. It happens when attention gets pulled along without you noticing.

When you do notice it, there's often a small pause. Nothing dramatic. Just a slight easing. The body settles a bit, not because you tell it to, but because the extra tension drops.

This doesn't happen straight away.

At first, you usually notice it late. You realise you've been lost in thought for a while before it clicks.

That still counts.

Every time you catch yourself like that, attention gets more familiar with how it drifts. Over time, noticing happens sooner. Not because you're trying harder, but because it becomes easier to recognise.

Surfing makes this obvious because waiting is unavoidable. When nothing's happening, the mind fills the space.

You don't need to stop that.

You just need to see it.

When mental activity is noticed, it often settles on its own. Not completely, not every time, but enough to stop it from running the show. Thoughts still come up, they just don't take over.

The same thing happens off the water. Waiting in line. Sitting in traffic. Pauses in conversation. The restlessness feels familiar.

Learning to notice it while surfing makes it easier to spot elsewhere.

The point isn't to control the mind.

It's to understand it.

When that understanding grows, waiting feels lighter. Even if nothing changes around you. The mind might still be busy, but it's no longer driving the moment.

One-Minute Practice

For one minute, just notice what the mind is doing.

Don't try to slow it down.

Don't try to follow it.

Don't try to push it away.

Notice thoughts as they show up.

Notice when attention gets pulled in.

Notice when you realise that's happened.

If the mind feels busy, notice that.

If it feels quiet, notice that.

When the minute is up, stop. No judging how it went.

5

THE BODY ON THE BOARD

Before thought kicks in, the body is already responding.

Sitting on the board, small adjustments are happening all the time. Weight shifts slightly. Legs reposition without any decision. Hands dip into the water, then lift. Balance is maintained through tiny movements you usually don't notice.

You're not deciding how to sit upright.

You're not calculating how to stay balanced.

The body responds to the movement of the water on its own.

This chapter is about noticing that responsiveness.

The body is often treated as something that needs fixing or controlling. People are taught to correct posture, manage tension, or hold themselves in a certain way. Attention gets directed toward adjusting what the body is doing.

In the water, that approach doesn't work very well.

The surface is always moving. Conditions keep changing. Trying to hold the body in a fixed position gets tiring fast.

Instead, the body adapts.

It shifts weight before the imbalance becomes obvious. It tightens and releases in small ways that keep you upright. These movements aren't planned. They're reactions.

Most of the time, you don't notice them.

You usually become aware of the body only when something goes wrong. Balance slips. A correction is needed. Suddenly, the body comes into focus.

This chapter invites you to notice sooner.

Not to interfere.

Just to notice.

You might feel pressure where the board meets your legs. You might sense subtle changes in balance as the water moves. You might notice tension in the shoulders or jaw, or a general sense of holding you weren't aware of before.

None of this needs fixing.

The body already knows how to respond to the water. When sensation is noticed without trying to change it, the body often moves more smoothly, not less.

That can feel counterintuitive.

A lot of people worry that paying attention to the body will make them stiff or awkward. They think awareness will interrupt automatic movement.

That only happens when attention turns into control.

When attention is just noticing, movement stays natural.

This difference matters.

Control slows things down. The body waits for instruction. Movements get bigger and clumsier. Responsiveness drops.

Noticing keeps responsiveness alive.

You're not telling the body what to do. You're letting it do what it already does, while seeing it more clearly.

This changes how sensation is experienced.

Take tension, for example. It's usually noticed only once it becomes uncomfortable. Shoulders creep up. The jaw tightens. The chest feels restricted. At that point, people often try to force relaxation.

That effort usually adds more tension.

When tension is noticed earlier, as a shift in sensation rather than a problem, it often changes on its own. The body adjusts without being told.

Nothing needs to be forced.

The body is already sensitive to the environment. It responds automatically to water temperature, movement, and instability. These responses are part of staying balanced.

Noticing them doesn't interrupt the process.

It reveals it.

This is especially clear when conditions change quickly.

A wobble. A sudden movement. The body reacts before thought catches up. Muscles engage. Breath shifts.

If attention is locked into thinking, the reaction can feel sudden or overwhelming. If attention is open to sensation, the same reaction feels continuous and manageable.

Not because the body does anything differently, but because attention isn't surprised by it.

Surprise is often what creates interference.

When sensation appears out of nowhere, attention tightens and the mind jumps in to explain or correct. Movement becomes less fluid.

When sensation is familiar, attention stays with it. The body keeps responding without interruption.

This familiarity doesn't come from constant monitoring.

It builds slowly, through repeated noticing.

You might notice the body clearly for a few seconds, then forget completely. You might realise later that you've been thinking and lost track of sensation.

That's normal.

Each return to sensation, no matter how brief, builds familiarity.

Over time, the body feels less like something you have to manage and more like something you can trust.

That trust isn't blind. It's based on seeing what actually happens.

You start to notice that balance is maintained through small, continuous adjustments, not through deliberate control.

Outside the water, the same thing is happening. Sitting in a chair. Standing in line. Walking down the street. The body is constantly adjusting.

Most of it goes unnoticed.

Noticing sensation in the water makes it easier to notice elsewhere. You begin to see how much is already being handled without instruction.

That recognition reduces the urge to interfere.

Intervening isn't always wrong. But when it happens automatically, it often creates more effort than needed.

The body doesn't need improvement to function.

It needs room to respond.

Attention plays a role here, not as a manager, but as a witness.

When attention witnesses sensation without trying to change it, responsiveness stays intact. When attention tries to control sensation, responsiveness drops.

This chapter isn't about perfect awareness of the body.

It's about noticing enough to trust what's already happening.

That trust grows slowly. It doesn't require discipline or constant effort. It develops through repeated recognition, especially in quiet moments.

Sitting on the board is one of those moments.

The water moves.

The body responds.

Attention notices, drifts, and returns.

That cycle is the practice.

One-Minute Practice

For one minute, notice bodily sensation.

You might notice pressure, balance, temperature, or tension.

Don't try to adjust posture.

Don't try to relax or correct anything.

Notice how the body responds to small movements in the water, or to your surroundings if you're on land.

If attention drifts into thought, notice when you realise that.

When the minute is over, stop. No judging how aware you were.

6

MISSING WAVES

Most surfers can remember waves they didn't take.

Maybe it was too far inside. Maybe it stood up faster than expected. Maybe hesitation showed up at the last second, and the moment passed.

Missing a wave usually feels different from falling off one. The body stays upright. The water stays calm. But something tightens inside.

Thoughts arrive quickly.

You should've gone.

You went too late.

You hesitated.

These reactions show up almost on their own.

This chapter isn't about fixing mistakes or making better decisions.

It's about noticing what happens around hesitation.

Hesitation isn't usually one clear moment. It's more like a short sequence.

First, attention narrows.

Then the body reacts.

Then, thought jumps in to explain what just happened.

By the time thought gets involved, the wave is already gone.

As a wave approaches, attention often moves ahead of the moment. It starts projecting. Speed. Size. Risk. Outcome. Most of this happens quietly, but it affects timing.

Sometimes paddling starts and then slows. Sometimes there's a half-second pause before moving. Sometimes effort comes on suddenly, without flow.

Those small delays matter.

What matters here isn't whether the choice was right or wrong.

It's whether the process is seen.

When hesitation goes unnoticed, it tends to carry over. The next wave comes with more tension. Attention tightens. The body becomes cautious. The mind starts watching itself.

That's often how one missed wave affects the next.

Not because the ocean changed, but because attention got caught in evaluation.

Most people respond by trying to do better next time. They replay the moment. They promise themselves they won't hesitate again.

That usually adds pressure.

This chapter points in a different direction.

Instead of focusing on the decision, it asks you to notice when attention shifts.

Often, hesitation shows up in the body first. A tightening in the chest or stomach. A slight change in breath. Muscles engaging without a clear direction.

These sensations appear before any story forms.

When they're noticed early, the moment stays simpler.

You might still take the wave.

You might still let it go.

But the extra layer of self-judgment doesn't land as hard.

Hesitation doesn't disappear.

It's part of surfing. Conditions change fast. Information is incomplete. Not every moment is clear.

What changes is your relationship to it.

When hesitation becomes familiar, it stops feeling like failure. It becomes a signal that attention has narrowed and the body is responding to uncertainty.

Signals don't need to be removed.

They need to be understood.

That understanding doesn't come from analysis. It comes from seeing the same pattern show up again and again.

You may notice hesitation appearing in similar situations. Certain sizes. Certain speeds. Certain crowd levels. Certain moods.

This isn't for strategy.

It's for recognition.

When hesitation is recognized as it arises, there's less urgency to react. The wave is still forming. The body is still responding. But there's less inner argument layered on top.

That reduction in internal noise matters more than making the perfect call.

Perfect decisions are rare.

Clean attention is not.

It also helps to notice what happens after a wave is missed.

Often, attention turns sharply inward. Thought starts replaying. The body tightens while the mind runs the moment again. What's happening now fades into the background.

That's another place to notice.

The wave is already gone. Replaying it doesn't bring it back. What it does do is shape what comes next.

If attention stays absorbed in evaluation, it's less available for the next moment.

Noticing that absorption is part of the practice.

You might realise you've been replaying a missed wave for a while. That realisation isn't too late. It interrupts the loop.

Nothing needs to be corrected. No positive thought is required.

Attention simply returns to what's here.

The water is still moving.

The body is still responding.

The horizon is still there.

This return isn't dramatic. It often feels flat or ordinary.

That ordinariness matters.

Surfing is full of moments that don't resolve neatly. Waves are missed. Timing shifts. The mind wants closure, but the ocean doesn't offer it.

Learning to stay with unfinished moments without adding extra tension is part of the learning.

Missed waves make this easy to see because they feel personal, even though the consequences are small.

Nothing has gone wrong. The session keeps going.

Over time, hesitation loses some of its charge. It still appears, but it doesn't take over as much.

That doesn't make surfing effortless.

It makes it less internally heavy.

The same pattern shows up elsewhere.

In conversations. At work. In relationships. Moments when action feels uncertain and hesitation arises.

Hesitation isn't just a surfing thing.

Learning to recognize it in the water makes it easier to see elsewhere, where the stakes may feel higher.

Again, the point isn't to eliminate hesitation.

It's to see it clearly enough that it doesn't multiply.

Missed waves become useful in this way.

Not because they teach you what to do next time, but because they show you what happens when attention tightens around uncertainty.

Seeing that is enough to begin loosening its grip.

One-Minute Practice

For one minute, notice moments of hesitation.

You might feel them in the body as tension or holding.

You might notice them in the mind as a delay or second-guessing.

Don't try to resolve the hesitation.

Don't decide whether it's justified.

Notice when it appears.

Notice what attention does around it.

If the moment has already passed and you realise it later, notice that realisation.

When the minute ends, simply return to what you were doing.

7

SHORT MOMENTS COUNT

A lot of people think attention only matters if it lasts a long time.

They assume that unless they can stay present or focused for minutes at a stretch, nothing useful is happening. Short moments get written off as not counting.

Surfing quietly proves otherwise.

Some of the most important moments in the water last only seconds. Sometimes less. A shift in balance. A change in position. A decision that happens before you have time to name it. These moments don't announce themselves. They come and go quickly.

Attention doesn't need to last a long time to matter.

It needs to arrive at the right moment.

This chapter is about noticing the value of short moments of awareness.

Surfing involves a lot of waiting, but when something happens, it happens fast. A wave rises. The body responds. The moment is gone. Whether you take the wave or not, the window for response is small.

Attention that waits for perfect clarity often arrives too late.

That doesn't mean attention has to be sharp or intense all the time. It means it doesn't need to be continuous to be useful.

Most surfers already understand this, even if they don't think of it this way. They trust brief flashes of readiness more than long stretches of thinking. They sense when something is about to happen without needing to explain it.

That sensing doesn't come from constant focus.

It comes from familiarity.

Familiarity lets attention recognize patterns quickly. It doesn't need to stay locked on. A brief moment of clarity is enough if it comes at the right time.

The problem starts when people dismiss these moments.

They notice something briefly, then ignore it because it didn't last. They assume that because attention drifted again, the moment didn't matter.

It did.

A moment of noticing doesn't lose its value just because it ends.

Each time attention recognizes itself, even briefly, familiarity grows. Over time, these moments become easier to notice and more frequent. Not because you're forcing them, but because attention knows what it's looking for.

Surfing gives plenty of chances to see this.

You might notice attention sharpen for a second as a set approaches, then soften again. You might feel a brief sense of alignment just before paddling, then lose it completely. You might notice tension appear and disappear within moments.

These aren't failures.

They're attention working as it does naturally.

The idea that attention has to be held continuously usually comes from places that value effort and persistence. In those settings, brief engagement is seen as not enough.

In surfing, that logic doesn't really apply.

Timing matters more than duration.

Attention that arrives for a second at the right moment is more useful than attention that's held without responsiveness. The water doesn't reward sustained concentration. It responds to presence.

That doesn't mean longer periods of awareness don't matter. They do. But they're not the only measure of attention, and they're not always the most important one.

Short moments matter because they interrupt habit.

Even a brief pause can change what happens next.

In the water, that might mean responding more smoothly to a wave. It might mean choosing not to paddle when something feels off. It might mean letting a wave go without added tension.

This can be reassuring, especially if distraction feels discouraging.

If you expect attention to stay steady, distraction feels like failure. If you see the value of brief noticing, distraction becomes part of the process.

You notice.

You lose it.

You notice again.

Nothing is missing.

This pattern isn't unique to surfing. It shows up in conversation, movement, and everyday decisions. Short moments of awareness appear, pass, and life keeps going.

The mistake is assuming that because these moments are brief, they don't matter.

In reality, they add up.

They build familiarity the same way small, repeated adjustments build balance. Gradually, without effort, attention becomes more responsive.

Surfing makes this obvious because it doesn't wait for you to be ready.

Waves come whether you're focused or distracted. The environment doesn't pause until attention settles. You respond as you are.

Short moments of noticing fit that reality.

It's also worth noticing how quickly judgment shows up.

You might notice attention for a second, then immediately think it wasn't enough. You might decide the moment was incomplete or pointless.

That judgment is just another movement of attention.

Seeing it is part of the practice.

The urge to hold onto or repeat a moment usually comes from misunderstanding its role. Attention doesn't need to last. It needs to be recognized.

Recognition changes the relationship to experience, even when it's brief.

Over time, this changes how you approach both waiting and action. You stop trying to hold attention in place. You stop measuring experience against an ideal.

Instead, you begin to trust that attention will show up when it's needed, if it's allowed to.

That trust doesn't feel like confidence.

It feels like ease.

Ease doesn't mean nothing goes wrong. It means less effort is spent trying to make moments last longer than they naturally do.

Short moments matter because they're honest.

They reflect how attention actually works.

Seeing their value removes a lot of unnecessary pressure, both in the water and outside it.

One-Minute Practice

For one minute, notice brief moments of clarity.

You might notice attention sharpen for a second, then drift away.

You might notice a quick recognition followed by thought.

Don't try to hold these moments.

Don't try to repeat them.

Notice when they appear.

Notice when they pass.

If attention is lost entirely and you realise it later, notice that realisation too.

When the minute is over, let it end and continue on.

8
LETTING WAVES GO

Not every wave is taken.

Sometimes the timing's off. Sometimes the shape isn't right. Sometimes the body tightens, and the moment passes. From the outside, it can look like nothing happened. Inside, there's often a lot going on.

Letting a wave go can feel light or heavy, depending on what attention does with the moment.

When letting go happens naturally, there's very little left behind. The wave passes. Attention returns to the water. The body settles back into waiting.

When letting go is followed by judgment, the moment sticks. Thought steps in to explain or defend the decision. Doubt shows up. Comparisons start.

This chapter isn't about choosing which waves to take.

It's about noticing what happens when a wave isn't taken.

There's an important difference between restraint and avoidance.

Restraint is responsive. It comes from sensing conditions as they are. Avoidance is reactive. It comes from discomfort with what might happen.

From the outside, they can look the same.

Inside, they feel very different.

Restraint feels quiet. The body stays relatively soft. Attention remains with the water. The moment ends cleanly.

Avoidance carries more weight. The body tightens. The breath shortens. Attention turns inward. Thought rushes in to justify not going. The wave is gone, but the moment doesn't feel finished.

You don't need to analyse this difference.

It shows up first in sensation.

You might notice a subtle holding in the chest or shoulders. A brief pause in the breath. A sharp turn of attention away from the water and toward explanation.

These signals appear before any clear thought.

When they're noticed early, the moment stays simpler.

This matters because surfing involves constant choice. Waves keep coming. Conditions change. Energy shifts. Not every opportunity needs to be acted on.

Trying to justify every decision creates unnecessary strain.

Letting waves go without explanation keeps attention available.

This doesn't mean stopping thought.

Thought often shows up after a wave is missed. It may compare your choice to someone else's. It may replay the moment. It may look for reasons.

That's normal.

The practice is noticing when attention gets caught in that process.

When attention is busy explaining, it's no longer with what's happening now. The next moment arrives while attention is still looking back.

Noticing that shift is enough to loosen it.

Letting waves go cleanly means letting the moment end.

That's harder than it sounds.

For many people, action feels easier than non-action. Going feels decisive. Not going can feel exposed. Uncertainty has more room to creep in.

Surfing brings this discomfort into the open.

Sometimes the most responsive choice is not to go. Sometimes the body senses something the mind can't yet explain. Sometimes energy is better conserved. Sometimes the moment just doesn't line up.

These moments don't need to be judged.

They need to be recognized and released.

Recognition allows release.

Judgment keeps the moment alive.

This doesn't mean restraint always feels calm. There can still be excitement or disappointment. The difference is that these feelings pass more quickly when they aren't wrapped in explanation.

Over time, letting waves go feels less personal.

The wave wasn't taken.

That's all.

Attention returns to waiting more easily. The body settles. The horizon hasn't changed.

This familiarity supports timing.

When attention isn't tangled in past decisions, it's more available for what's coming next. Responsiveness improves, not because choices are better, but because attention isn't split.

The same pattern shows up outside the water.

There are plenty of moments in daily life where action is possible but not taken. A comment left unsaid. A choice delayed. An opportunity passed.

Often, these moments are followed by internal commentary.

Should you have acted?

Did you miss something?

What does it say about you?

That commentary keeps attention busy long after the moment has passed.

Seeing this in surfing makes it easier to spot elsewhere.

Letting go without explanation isn't indifference.

It's responsiveness without unnecessary attachment.

Attachment shows up as lingering attention.

When attention lingers, energy gets tied up maintaining a story. When attention releases, that energy becomes available again.

This doesn't mean reflection is never useful. Sometimes, review and learning matter.

But review is different from rumination.

Review happens later, when there's space. Rumination happens in the middle of things, pulling attention away from what's happening now.

Learning to let moments end reduces rumination.

That reduction doesn't come from discipline. It comes from seeing how quickly explanation appears, and how little it adds in the moment.

The water keeps moving.

The next set approaches. Conditions shift. Attention is needed again.

Letting the previous moment end fully is part of staying available.

This availability isn't dramatic.

It feels ordinary.

That ordinariness is a sign that attention is no longer over-involved.

One-Minute Practice

For one minute, notice moments of non-action.

You might notice a decision not to move.

You might notice a pause where action could have happened.

Notice what the body does as the moment passes.

Notice whether attention lingers or releases.

If an explanation shows up, notice that.

If attention returns to the present easily, notice that too.

When the minute is over, let the moment finish and move on.

9
FORGETTING AND REMEMBERING

Forgetting isn't a mistake.

In the water, attention drifts all the time. It wanders into thought. It follows memory. It runs through what just happened or what might happen next. Minutes can pass before you realise attention has gone somewhere else.

That's normal.

A lot of people think practice means staying attentive. When attention slips, they take it as a failure. They think they should have noticed sooner or stayed present longer.

That assumption creates unnecessary pressure.

Attention doesn't stay in one place. It moves. Forgetting is part of how it moves.

This chapter is about noticing the moment of remembering.

Forgetting happens quietly. Attention gets absorbed without announcing itself. Remembering is different. It shows up as a small interruption. A sudden realisation.

You notice that you weren't paying attention.

That moment matters more than all the time spent forgetting before it.

When people fixate on forgetting, they miss this. They judge themselves for being distracted. They focus on how long attention was gone. They try to stop it from happening again.

In doing that, they overlook the fact that remembering has already happened.

Remembering is attention recognising itself.

It doesn't have to happen quickly to matter. Even if attention was lost for a long time, the moment you notice it changes everything.

In that moment, attention is back.

Nothing else is required.

In the water, this often happens while waiting. You might suddenly realise you've been replaying a wave or imagining the next set. The realisation arrives on its own. For a brief moment, attention is clear.

That clarity doesn't need to last.

Trying to hold onto it usually adds effort and tension. The moment passes naturally.

The value lies in the recognition, not in how long it lasts.

Over time, these moments of remembering add up. Attention starts to recognise its own movements more easily. Forgetting still happens, but remembering comes sooner.

Not because you're trying harder, but because attention is becoming familiar with itself.

Surfing makes this easy to see because forgetting often happens in stillness. There's nothing external to anchor attention. The mind fills the space. When remembering happens, the contrast is clear.

You notice the sound of the water again. The feel of the board. The horizon. The body sitting upright.

That return doesn't need to be highlighted. Noticing it is enough.

Some people expect remembering to feel good or rewarding. They look for a sense of progress or success. When it feels ordinary instead, they dismiss it.

That ordinariness is a good sign.

If remembering felt dramatic every time, it would turn into something to chase. Attention would start looking for the feeling rather than recognising itself.

In reality, remembering often feels neutral.

That neutrality allows it to happen again and again without becoming a goal.

Forgetting and remembering aren't opposites. They're part of the same cycle. Attention drifts. It gets absorbed. It realizes it's absorbed. Then it moves again.

Trying to eliminate forgetting breaks this cycle. It turns attention into something to control rather than something to understand.

Understanding comes from letting the cycle play out.

This doesn't only happen in the water.

In conversation, you might lose track of what you were saying and then realise it. While walking, you drift into thought and then notice your surroundings again. At work, attention jumps ahead and then returns.

Each time remembering happens, attention is present.

The time spent forgetting doesn't cancel that.

When people judge forgetting, they often miss remembering altogether. They focus on the absence instead of the return.

This chapter asks you to shift that focus.

Instead of asking how long attention stayed, notice how often it came back.

Each return is recognition.

Recognition grows through repetition, not through effort. Forgetting still happens, but it becomes less discouraging. You stop measuring practice by duration.

You start to see that attention works in brief appearances.

In the water, this can be a relief. Waiting no longer needs to be filled with steady awareness. Forgetting is allowed. Remembering is enough.

This allowance reduces strain.

With less strain, attention returns more easily. Not because it's forced, but because it isn't being resisted.

Forgetting feels less personal. Remembering becomes more common.

This shift is quiet. It doesn't announce itself. It just changes how waiting feels.

The water is the same.

The body is the same.

Attention still moves as it always has.

What changes is your relationship to forgetting.

One-Minute Practice

For one minute, let attention do whatever it does.

It might drift.

QUINN PATH

You might forget completely.

When you realise attention has been elsewhere, notice that realisation.

Don't rush to return to anything.

Don't try to stay present.

Let remembering happen when it happens.

When the minute is over, leave the experience as it is and continue.

10

THE MOMENT BEFORE PADDLING

There's a brief moment before action when everything gathers.

The wave approaches. Speed builds. The body leans forward slightly. Attention narrows. There's no time to think things through. Whatever happens next happens fast.

Every surfer knows this moment.

It's also where fear shows up most clearly.

Fear doesn't arrive as one clear feeling. It comes as a set of changes. The body tightens. The breath shortens. Attention locks onto what might happen next.

Often, excitement shows up at the same time.

These two aren't as different as they seem. Both involve heightened sensitivity. Both carry extra energy. Both pull attention forward.

This chapter isn't about getting rid of fear or managing it.

It's about noticing what happens in that moment.

Fear is often talked about as something to overcome. Push through it. Calm it down. Replace it with confidence.

That assumes fear is a problem.

In practice, fear is information.

It shows up when something matters. It sharpens perception. It prepares the body to respond. The issue isn't fear itself. The issue is being caught off guard by it.

When fear arrives unexpectedly, attention tightens even more. The body reacts quickly. Thought rushes in to keep up. Timing gets distorted. You act too early, too late, or with hesitation.

When fear is familiar, it still shows up.

It just has less power to disrupt.

Familiarity changes the relationship.

One of the first things fear affects is breathing.

As the wave approaches, the breath often becomes shallow. The chest tightens. The rhythm shortens. This happens automatically, before any decision is made.

Trying to fix the breath in that moment rarely helps. There usually isn't time. Effort adds tension. Attention splits.

What does help is noticing the change as it begins.

When fear is recognised early, the change in breathing is recognised early too. The breath may still shorten, but it doesn't arrive as a shock. There's less urgency piled on top of it.

The body doesn't need to be calmed.

It needs to be understood.

Understanding doesn't mean analysis.

It means noticing the order in which things happen.

First, attention narrows.

Then the body reacts.

Then thought tries to explain.

By the time thought gets involved, the moment has already passed.

This sequence is easy to miss because it happens so quickly. Surfing makes it obvious because commitment can't be delayed.

You either paddle or you don't.

The moment before paddling isn't a place for careful decision-making. There's no time to weigh options. Action comes from sensing and response, not reasoning.

When attention gets caught in fear stories, the response loses flow. You might hesitate, then overcommit. You might rush. You might act out of urgency rather than timing.

When attention recognises fear as it appears, there's more continuity. The body still reacts. The breath still changes. But fewer extra reactions pile on.

This doesn't guarantee a better outcome.

Waves are unpredictable. Conditions shift. Mistakes still happen.

What changes is the quality of the moment.

The moment feels cleaner.

Fear may still be there. The heart may still race. The body may still feel tense. But there's less added tension from fighting or explaining what's happening.

That matters because extra reactions cost energy.

Panic isn't fear. Panic is fear mixed with surprise and resistance. When fear is expected, panic has less room to take hold.

Surfing brings you back to this moment again and again. Over time, fear becomes familiar. Not because it disappears, but because it's recognised sooner.

Recognising sooner creates space. Not a pause that needs filling, just a moment without interference.

The body responds more fluidly when it isn't being overridden. Attention stays closer to sensation. Timing improves naturally.

This isn't something you practise deliberately.

It develops through repeated noticing.

The same pattern shows up outside the water.

Moments of commitment happen everywhere. Speaking up. Stepping back. Acting without certainty. Fear appears. Breathing changes. Attention narrows.

The sequence is the same.

Seeing it clearly in surfing makes it easier to recognise elsewhere.

Noticing fear doesn't mean acting without it.

It means fear doesn't have to carry you away.

That difference is subtle, but it matters.

Fear doesn't need to be removed to be workable.

It just needs to be familiar.

The moment before paddling makes that clear.

One-Minute Practice

For one minute, recall a recent moment of commitment.

Notice what happened in the body.

Notice how attention narrowed.

Notice how the breath changed.

Don't try to recreate the feeling.

Don't try to calm it.

Just notice the sequence as you remember it.

If fear or excitement shows up now, notice that too.

When the minute ends, let the memory fade and return to what's here.

11

WHEN NOTHING IS HAPPENING

After the intensity of action, there's often a long stretch where nothing develops.

The water settles. Sets thin out. The horizon stays empty. Time seems to slow down.

These moments can feel harder than the waves themselves.

When nothing is happening, attention doesn't have much to do. There's no decision to make. No movement to respond to. No urgency to grab onto.

This is usually when restlessness shows up.

Thoughts start wandering. Impatience builds. The body can feel heavier. You might start wondering whether you're in the wrong spot, whether conditions are changing, or whether the session is worth it.

This chapter is about noticing what happens when there's nothing to respond to.

When attention has no clear object, it often turns inward. It looks for something to engage with. It fills the space with commentary.

That's not a problem. It's just what attention does when it isn't needed.

The discomfort that comes up in these moments doesn't come from the lack of waves.

It comes from resisting the lack of stimulation.

There's often an unspoken expectation that something should be happening.

When that expectation isn't met, tension shows up.

You might notice subtle tightening in the body. The breath may get shallow or uneven. Attention may jump quickly from one thought to the next.

None of this needs fixing.

What matters is whether it's noticed.

When restlessness goes unnoticed, it tends to build. Thought speeds up. The body settles less. Waiting starts to feel heavy and pointless.

When restlessness is noticed, it often softens.

Not because it's pushed away, but because the extra layer of resistance drops.

Waiting doesn't need to be filled.

That's easy to say and harder to feel.

Modern life doesn't leave much room for empty time. Screens, tasks, and conversations constantly pull attention outward. The water, by contrast, offers long stretches where there's nothing to do but wait.

At first, that can feel uncomfortable.

It's also revealing.

When nothing is happening, attention shows its habits clearly. You see how quickly it looks for stimulation. You see how uneasy stillness can feel.

Seeing this is part of the practice.

You might notice how often you check the horizon even though nothing has changed. You might feel an urge to paddle somewhere else without a clear reason. You might notice the mind spinning stories about what could happen next.

These aren't mistakes.

They're information.

They show how attention behaves when it isn't being used.

When attention is allowed to be as it is in these moments, something shifts over time. Waiting feels less charged. Time feels less heavy. The urge to fill the space weakens.

That doesn't mean waiting becomes enjoyable.

It means it becomes simpler.

Simplicity here doesn't come from effort.

It comes from allowing the moment to be incomplete.

Nothing is happening, and that's allowed.

This allowance has real effects.

When attention isn't busy fighting waiting, it's more available when something finally does develop. There's less scrambling. Less urgency. Less sense of being dragged out of stillness.

Responsiveness improves because attention hasn't been scattered.

This pattern shows up clearly in daily life too.

Waiting for a reply. Sitting in traffic. Pausing between tasks. These moments trigger the same restlessness and mental activity.

Learning to notice waiting in the water makes it easier to recognise it elsewhere.

You begin to see that the discomfort isn't caused by inactivity itself, but by the expectation that something should be happening.

Letting go of that expectation changes how the moment feels.

The water is honest about this. It doesn't reward impatience. Paddling around aimlessly doesn't make waves arrive faster. Checking again and again doesn't change anything.

The only option is to wait.

Waiting doesn't have to be passive. It can be attentive without being busy.

Attentive waiting means noticing what's present without needing it to change.

That includes boredom, impatience, and dullness.

These states are usually avoided or judged. Here, they can just be seen.

Seeing them doesn't make them disappear right away.

It keeps them from turning into extra tension.

Over time, the fear of nothing happening eases.

Empty moments become easier to sit with.

This comfort isn't dramatic.

It feels neutral.

That neutrality lets attention stay open.

When something finally appears on the horizon, attention responds naturally, without needing to recover from restlessness.

This chapter brings the book back to where it started.

Between sets, nothing seems to be happening.

But internally, a lot is being revealed.

Noticing this quietly changes how waiting feels, in the water and elsewhere.

One-Minute Practice

For one minute, notice waiting.

Don't look for anything to happen.

Don't try to make the minute interesting.

Notice restlessness if it shows up.

Notice impatience or dullness.

If attention drifts into thought, notice when you realise that.

When the minute ends, let waiting continue without comment.

12
WHAT CARRIES OVER

At some point, it becomes obvious that what you notice in the water doesn't stay there.

The same patterns show up elsewhere, often more quietly. Waiting. Hesitation. Fear. Restlessness. Moments of readiness that arrive out of nowhere. Moments of distraction you don't notice until later.

Surfing makes these things easy to see because the setting is simple. Fewer choices. Fewer distractions. Clear consequences. Attention doesn't have much room to hide.

Daily life is messier.

There are more demands, more interruptions, more reasons to stay busy. Because of that, attention's movements blend into routines. They're easier to miss.

What carries over isn't a method or a technique.

It's familiarity.

You start to recognize the same sequences outside the water. Attention narrows when something matters. The body reacts before thought kicks in. Fear changes the breath. Hesitation shows up as holding. Restlessness appears when nothing is happening.

None of this feels surprising anymore.

That lack of surprise makes a difference.

When attention recognises what's happening early, there's less interference. Fear may still be there, but it doesn't escalate as fast. Hesitation may still appear, but it doesn't turn into self-judgment. Restlessness may still surface, but it doesn't require immediate action.

This doesn't mean life becomes smooth.

Situations are still uncertain. Outcomes are still unpredictable. The change is how much extra strain is added.

A lot of difficulty in daily life doesn't come from events themselves, but from what gets layered on top. Anticipation. Resistance. Explanation. Self-evaluation. All of that costs energy.

The familiarity developed through surfing reduces some of this layering.

Not all of it.

Enough of it.

You begin to notice when attention is rushing ahead of the moment. You notice when thought is replaying something that's already over. You notice when the body has tightened in response to uncertainty.

These notices don't fix anything.

They stop things from escalating.

That's often more useful than solving problems.

Most problems don't explode instantly. They build. When escalation slows down, there's more room to respond. More options. Less pressure.

The practices in this book aren't about creating calm. Calm might show up sometimes, but it isn't the goal.

What matters is clarity.

Clarity lets fear be present without taking over. It lets waiting exist without becoming heavy. It lets action happen without forcing it.

Over time, this changes how effort feels.

Less energy goes into managing what's happening inside. More energy is available for responding to what's actually in front of you. The change is subtle, but it adds up.

You might notice you recover more quickly from difficult moments. Hesitation doesn't hang around as long. Fear appears and passes without leaving as much behind.

These aren't achievements.

They're signs of familiarity.

Familiarity grows quietly. It doesn't announce progress or require new beliefs. It's simply a clearer understanding of how attention already works.

Surfing keeps offering reminders.

Every session includes waiting, action, fear, and release. Each session reinforces what's already been seen. There's no final lesson to extract.

The water doesn't reward conclusions.

Neither does life.

Moments that require attention keep showing up, often without warning. The value of what you've learned isn't that you apply it deliberately. It's that attention recognises itself more easily when it matters.

That recognition doesn't belong to surfing.

Surfing was just a clear place to notice it.

You don't need to bring anything special into daily life.

You don't need to practise differently.

The same movements of attention are already there.

What changes is that you see them.

Recognition reduces interference.

Less interference allows responsiveness.

That responsiveness is what carries over.

Nothing needs to be added.

The patterns were already in place.

You've just learned to notice them.

One-Minute Practice

For one minute, notice attention outside the water.

You might notice it while standing, sitting, or moving.

You might notice fear, hesitation, restlessness, or readiness. Don't look for anything specific.

Just notice how attention behaves on its own.

If you forget and realise it later, notice that realisation.

When the minute ends, let the day continue as it is.

13

STAYING WITH WHAT IS

The water doesn't offer closure.

Sessions end, but the same patterns keep showing up. Waiting comes back. Fear comes back. Moments of readiness appear and fade. Attention drifts. Remembering happens. Nothing resolves once and for all.

That isn't a problem.

It's a clear picture of how attention actually works.

Nothing new has been added in this book. No special skill has been layered on top of experience. What's changed, slowly, is familiarity. Familiarity with how attention moves. Familiarity with how fear shows up. Familiarity with how the body responds before thought has time to comment.

It shows up as less interference.

Less interference means fewer extra reactions added to moments as they unfold. Less urgency piled onto fear. Less weight added to hesitation. Less resistance around waiting. The moments themselves don't disappear. What eases is the struggle around them.

Surfing makes this easy to see because it strips things down.

There's water. A board. A body. Attention. Conditions change without warning. Timing matters. Fear shows up honestly. There's nowhere to hide from what's happening.

In daily life, the same patterns are there, but they're easier to miss. Distraction is constant. Activity fills the space. Attention jumps from one thing to the next without pause.

What carries over from the water is the recognition that attention behaves the same way everywhere.

It narrows when something matters.

It drifts when nothing is required.

It reacts before thought explains.

Seeing this reduces surprise, and that changes a lot.

When fear is no longer unexpected, it doesn't escalate as quickly. When hesitation is noticed early, it doesn't multiply. When restlessness is seen as a response to emptiness, it loses some of its grip.

None of this requires effort.

Effort would just add another layer.

The practices in this book were kept brief on purpose. They weren't meant to build endurance or force focus. They were meant to point attention back to what was already happening.

Short moments of noticing are enough.

They interrupt habit.

They soften reaction.

They build familiarity.

Over time, these moments add up—as understanding.

Understanding changes how experience feels.

Not dramatically.

Not permanently.

Just enough.

You may still have sessions where fear feels strong. You may still hesitate. You may still miss waves. You may still sit through long stretches where the mind stays busy.

Nothing has gone wrong when that happens.

Those moments are part of the same process.

The difference is that you're less likely to be carried away by them. You recognize what's happening sooner. You return to what's present with less effort.

That return isn't something you do.

It happens on its own when interference drops.

The water will keep offering chances to see this. So will everyday life. Conversations, decisions, delays, commitments. They all carry the same structure.

Attention moves.

It gets absorbed.

It recognizes itself.

There's no final state to reach.

Staying with what is doesn't mean staying still. It means letting experience unfold without unnecessary correction. It means trusting responsiveness more than control.

Surfing doesn't reward forcing.

Neither does attention.

If this book has done anything, it's pointed back to what was already there.

Between sets.

Before paddling.

When nothing is happening.

And in the moments that follow you back onto land.

One-Minute Practice

For one minute, notice what's already here.

You might notice sensations, thoughts, or movements.

You might notice attention drifting and returning.

Don't treat this as practice.

Don't try to conclude anything.

When the minute ends, let it end and continue with your day.

Nothing more needs to be done.

14
A NOTE TO READERS

If you've spent some time with this book, I'd appreciate hearing what you noticed.

Not as a rating or a judgment on whether it worked, but simply as a reflection. What felt familiar. What stayed with you? What didn't?

If you choose to leave a review or share a few thoughts wherever you found this book, it helps other readers decide whether this way of looking at attention might be useful for them too.

Thanks for reading, and for taking these observations with you into the water and into daily life.

www.ingramcontent.com/pod-product-compliance
Lightning Source LLC
Chambersburg PA
CBHW060506080526
44584CB00015B/1563